Festivals *of the* World

PUERTO RICO

Gareth Stevens Publishing
MILWAUKEE

Written by
ERIN FOLEY

Edited by
ELIZABETH BERG

Designed by
JAILANI BASARI

First published in North America in 1997 by
Gareth Stevens Publishing
1555 North RiverCenter Drive, Suite 201
Milwaukee, Wisconsin 53212 USA

For a free color catalog describing Gareth
Stevens' list of high-quality books and multimedia
programs, call
1-800-542-2595 (USA)
or 1-800-461-9120 (Canada).
Gareth Stevens Publishing's Fax: (414) 225-0377.
See our catalog, too, on the World Wide Web:
http://gsinc.com

© TIMES EDITIONS PTE LTD 1997
REPRINTED 1999
Originated and designed by
Times Books International
an imprint of Times Editions Pte Ltd
Times Centre, 1 New Industrial Road
Singapore 536196
Printed in Singapore

Library of Congress Catqaloging-in-Publication Data
Foley, Erin.
Puerto Rico / by Erin Foley.
p. cm. — (Festivals of the world)
Includes bibliographical references (p. 27)
and index.
Summary: Describes how the culture of Puerto
Rico is reflected in its festivals.
ISBN 0-8368-1687-0
1. Festivals—Puerto Rico—Juvenile literature.
2. Puerto Rico—Social life and customs—Juvenile
literature. I. Series.
GT4828.A2P84 1997
394.2'697295—DC20 96-33573

2 3 4 5 6 7 8 9 03 02 01 00 99

CONTENTS

It's Festival Time . . .

The word for festival or party in Spanish is *fiesta* [fee-AYS-tah], and Puerto Ricans sure know a lot about parties. Even streets have their own patron saint's festival, and Christmas goes on for two months! Get ready for the feasting and dancing and partying to go on all night. You may think this is a little island, but Puerto Ricans have some of the best music in the world. They're also great dancers. So put on your party dress, and follow the music to the plaza. It's festival time in Puerto Rico . . .

WHERE'S PUERTO RICO?

Puerto Rico is one of the warm, mountainous islands that make up the West Indies. The island faces the Atlantic Ocean to the north, while the sparkling blue Caribbean Sea laps against its southern and eastern coasts. Puerto Rico is the only Spanish colony that never declared its independence, although a few unsuccessful rebellions were attempted. Today, it is a commonwealth of the United States. Its people are U.S. citizens, but they cannot vote in presidential elections.

Who are the Puerto Ricans?

Two Puerto Rican girls are dressed for *bomba y plena* dancing. Find out all about it on page 14.

The first people to live in Puerto Rico were the **Taino** people. When the Spanish came to the New World, they forced the Tainos to work for them almost as slaves. After a short time, there were hardly any Tainos left—they had almost all died from overwork, disease brought by the Europeans, and rebellions. The Spanish then brought in African slaves to work for them. As the years passed, all these people blended together. Today, almost all Puerto Ricans have some Spanish, African, and Native Puerto Rican blood in them.

Their culture is also a mixture of these three, along with a strong influence from their large neighbor, the United States. Many Puerto Ricans have moved to the United States in the hope of finding a better life. There are now almost as many Puerto Ricans in the United States as there are in Puerto Rico.

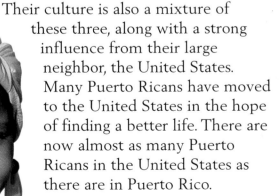

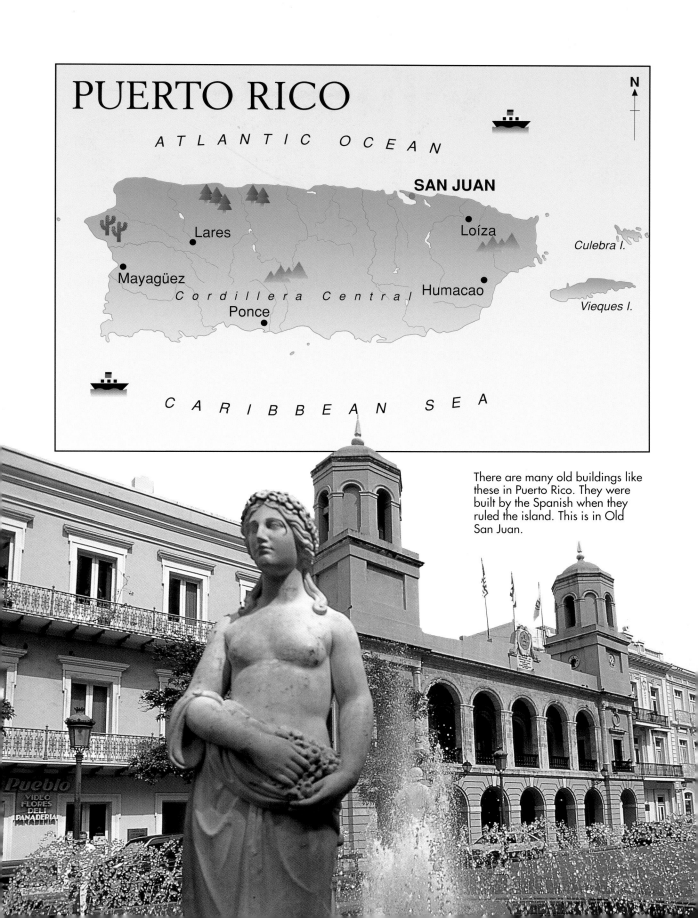

PUERTO RICO

N

ATLANTIC OCEAN

SAN JUAN

Lares

Loíza

Culebra I.

Mayagüez

Cordillera Central

Humacao

Vieques I.

Ponce

CARIBBEAN SEA

There are many old buildings like these in Puerto Rico. They were built by the Spanish when they ruled the island. This is in Old San Juan.

Pueblo
VIDEO
FLORES
DELI
PANADERIA

WHEN'S THE FIESTA?

SPRING

- ✪ **EMANCIPATION DAY**—Celebrates the abolition of slavery.
- ✪ **HOLY WEEK AND EASTER**
- ✪ **PABLO CASALS MUSIC FESTIVAL**—Classical musicians come from all over the world to perform in the largest musical event in the Caribbean.

Come dance with me for Santiago Apostol on page 14.

SUMMER

- ✪ **FEAST OF SAN JUAN BAUTISTA** The biggest beach party of the year. At midnight, people walk backwards into the ocean to greet St. John the Baptist, patron saint of San Juan and of Puerto Rico.
- ✪ **LUIZ MUÑOZ RIVERA'S BIRTHDAY**—Celebrates the man who negotiated Puerto Rico's independence from Spain.
- ✪ **COMMONWEALTH CONSTITUTION DAY**—Marks the start of the U.S. invasion of Puerto Rico and celebrates its commonwealth status.
- ✪ **PUERTO RICAN DAY**

FALL

- ✪ **GRITO DE LARES**
- ✪ **PUERTO RICO DAY OF DISCOVERY**—Celebrates Christopher Columbus' arrival on the island.
- ✪ **FEAST OF OUR LADY OF MONSERRATE**—Pilgrims come to Hormigueros to honor Our Lady. They climb the stone stairs of the cathedral on their knees.

WINTER

- ✪ **ST. NICHOLAS DAY** ✪ **CHRISTMAS**
- ✪ **FIESTA DE LOS INOCENTES** ✪ **NEW YEAR'S DAY**
- ✪ **THREE KINGS DAY** ✪ **OCTAVITAS**
- ✪ **CANDELARIA DAY**—Families burn a piece of wood in the community bonfire to protect their house from fire during the year.
- ✪ **FIESTA CALLE SAN SEBASTIÁN**

Grab a costume and come to los Inocentes on page 21.

7

CALLE SAN SEBASTIÁN

There are hundreds of **patron saints**' festivals in Puerto Rico. Every town has its patron saint festival, sometimes several. Festivals usually begin about 10 days before the actual saint's day. The streets of the town fill with stalls offering special foods, and the central plaza fills with music and dancing. There are also games of chance, Ferris wheels, and carousels. People come from miles around to join in the fun. But the festival isn't just for having fun. It's also a time to honor the town's patron saint. On the Sunday closest to the official date, four people carry a wooden image of the saint around the town in a special procession. Mass, or church service, is held twice a day during the festival period.

Musical performances are part of the Calle San Sebastián festival. Puerto Rico is well known for its contributions to classical music, as well as jazz and pop.

Calle San Sebastián Festival

A procession, shows, music and dancing, crafts, and horse shows—the festival for San Sebastián Street in Old San Juan has it all. Calle San Sebastián has a patron saint's day all for itself, and they make quite a party of it. The neighborhood streets become choked with people. Bands of musicians march through the streets, strumming Puerto Rican folk music on guitars, or blowing up dance rhythms with brass horns and drums.

An impromptu parade makes its way down Calle San Sebastián.

Come to a horse show

Clowns are part of the fun at the Calle San Sebastián festival.

Horse shows are a special part of this street fiesta. **Paso Fino** horses have been bred in the Caribbean for a long time, and Puerto Ricans are very proud of them. The name *Paso Fino* means "fine pace." Their step is supposed to be so graceful that the rider can carry a full glass of water without spilling a drop.

Listen to the music . . .

A big part of Puerto Rican festivals is the music. The most famous kind of Puerto Rican music is **salsa**. *Salsa* means "sauce." You probably know salsa if you've eaten Mexican food—it's the spicy sauce that you dip your tortilla chips in. Puerto Ricans call this music *salsa* because it's a blend of styles, like a sauce. Musicians took the percussion sound of traditional Afro-Caribbean music and combined it with the sound of big band jazz, creating a rhythm that makes your feet dance.

Think about this
Most Puerto Ricans are Catholic, but you can see the influence of the religions of the Taino and West African peoples in Puerto Rican festivals today. Saints' days are a Catholic tradition, but the way they are celebrated is typically Puerto Rican.

A beat to make you dance

Salsa has become one of the favorite dance rhythms around the world. Some of the most famous salsa musicians include Tito Puente, Gilberto Santarrosa, Willie Colón, and from Panama, Ruben Blades. Menudo is the favorite of the young people. A typical band includes a vocalist and chorus, a piano, a bass, a horn section, and a lot of percussion instruments, such as bongos, congas, maracas, timbales, claves, and cowbells.

Music and dance are the most important ingredients in Puerto Rican festivals.

SANTIAGO APOSTOL

Near the end of July, the coastal town of Loíza (find it on the map on page 5—it's near San Juan) fills with a carnival atmosphere. People walk around in fancy costumes with devilish masks. Caribbean rhythms fill the air, and colorful parades occupy the streets. The fiesta for Santiago Apostol [san-tee-AH-go ah-pohs-TOHL], St. James the Apostle, is one of the most colorful festivals in Puerto Rico. It combines traditions of the three cultures that make up Puerto Rico today: African, Spanish, and Taino. Most of the people living in Loíza are descended from African slaves. Over the centuries, this festival has kept alive many of the traditions of the African ancestors of the residents of Loíza. Some of the costumes even reflect Puerto Rico's Taino heritage.

The devil masks worn for the Fiesta of Santiago Apostol look very much like the masks made by the African ancestors of today's Puerto Ricans.

Who is Santiago Apostol?

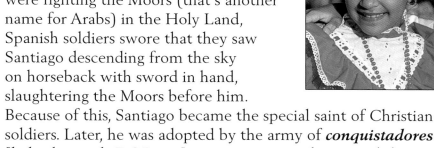

These two children are wearing traditional Puerto Rican dress for the Santiago festival.

Many centuries ago, when Europeans were fighting the Moors (that's another name for Arabs) in the Holy Land, Spanish soldiers swore that they saw Santiago descending from the sky on horseback with sword in hand, slaughtering the Moors before him. Because of this, Santiago became the special saint of Christian soldiers. Later, he was adopted by the army of *conquistadores* [kohn-kees-tah-DOR-ays], or conquerors, who carried their religion to the New World. But that's not the end of Santiago's adventures.

A procession of devils and dancers passes the cathedral.

Santiago goes African

In the New World, the Spanish colonists refused to allow the **Yoruba** slaves from West Africa to worship their own god, Shango. Shango was their all-powerful god of thunder, lightning, and war. In pictures of a warlike Santiago descending from the clouds, the Africans saw a resemblance to Shango. So they continued to worship Shango, disguised as Santiago. Today, Puerto Rico's Santiago is a mixture of Spanish conquistador and Yoruba war god.

Dancing along

For nine days before the fiesta for Santiago Apostol, people honor Santiago by gathering to say prayers. On July 25, there is a big procession in honor of Santiago. The procession sways and dances to the sounds of salsa music and traditional **bomba y plena** rhythms. In the bomba y plena, a dancer and a drummer perform a "give and take" of rhythm and dance, while a soloist and chorus sing along. This dance, which blends African and Hispanic dance styles, started in the coastal town of Ponce. It is a uniquely Puerto Rican tradition.

The bomba y plena is a special Puerto Rican invention that combines Spanish and African styles to make something totally new.

Devils and Christians

There is one part of the festival called "The Devils against the Christians." People dress in fancy costumes with masks and painted faces. Some wear brightly colored clothes and white masks. They are the Spanish *caballeros* [cah-bah-YAY-rohs], or men on horseback. Others dress as **vejigantes** [vay-hee-GAHN-tays] to represent the Moors. They wear devil masks made from painted coconut shells with long horns along the top or sides. There are also other costumes for Santiago. Some men dress as clowns or as crazy women, called *locas*. The locas blacken their faces, wear mismatched clothes, and often act silly or pretend to sweep the streets and porches as they go along.

Some vejigantes ready to scare you into good behavior.

LAS NAVIDADES

D uring the Christmas season, or *las Navidades* [lahs nah-vee-DAH-days], Puerto Ricans pull out all the stops with their merry-making. Relatives and friends arrive from the mainland United States, laden with gifts and good wishes for residents of **la Isla** [lah EES-lah], as Puerto Ricans fondly call their homeland.

Putting up the lights

The Christmas season officially begins on Saint Nicholas Day, which is on December 15. People prepare for the holiday season by putting up beautifully detailed nativity scenes, Christmas trees, and colored lights. Nativity scenes are a Puerto Rican tradition. Sometimes they are very elaborate. Christmas trees are a more recent addition. Christmas lights are also a big part of a Puerto Rican Christmas. People deck their houses, front yards, windows, and balconies with impressive displays of lights, which shine all night long. Sometimes whole neighborhoods join together to create elaborate decorations.

Left: Santa Claus is not native to Puerto Rico, but he has become popular through the U.S. influence.

Opposite: Christmas parades are popular. Here one marches down a San Juan street.

The Christmas feast includes roast pig. Early in the day, they place the pig over an open pit. They turn it on a spit over the fire for several hours until it is fully cooked and the skin is crunchy. Every part of the pig is eaten with great relish, down to the knuckles and feet.

Cuatro groups

The traditional music of Puerto Rico is performed by *cuatro* groups. These groups take their name from the cuatro, a small Puerto Rican guitar with four strings. It used to be a tradition for small bands of musicians to travel from town to town throughout the holiday season, singing folksongs. They still play at the early morning masses celebrated during the nine days before Christmas eve.

You might see a cuatro group singing and playing as they stroll down the street at Christmastime.

18

Waking up the neighbors

A long-standing Puerto Rican tradition is the ***parranda*** [pah-RHAN-dah], in which a small group of people gathers to visit friends and sing to them. The special holiday songs they sing celebrate Christmas, family, and good times. The parranda musicians sing boisterously and even bang on pots and pans for extra noise. Revelers also surprise their friends with ***asaltos*** [ah-SAL-tohs], an unexpected form of the parranda—often waking them late at night and demanding to be let into the house, where they are given food and drink. After singing together, they try to persuade their friends to join them in surprising others. As the night wears on, the group grows larger, noisier, and merrier. The traveling party can continue until all hours of the morning.

Parrandas may start with a handful of people and continue until the whole town has joined in.

19

AROUND CHRISTMAS

Christmas is the high point of the Puerto Rican year. In fact, Puerto Ricans like Christmas so much that they don't want it to end, so they go on celebrating right through to January 15th! The season is filled with celebrations of different parts of the Christmas story, and each of these celebrations has its own traditions.

Los Inocentes

On December 28, Christmas has just ended. Time to take a break from holiday festivities? No, not in Puerto Rico—it's time for another festival! This is the *Dia de los Inocentes* [DEE-ah day lohs ee-noh-SAIN-tays], the Day of the Innocents. Do you know the story from the Bible? King Herod wanted to get rid of the Christ child, so he ordered that all male children under 2 years old be killed. This festival honors the memory of the children who were killed.

On los Inocentes, people dress up in costumes like this one. The costume completely covers them. Whole groups sometimes all dress the same.

Kidnapping the boys

Los Inocentes is like a big carnival. The traditional celebration was for men to dress up as Herod's evil soldiers and go house to house. At each house, they would "kidnap" the oldest boy from the family. To get their children back, the families had to offer the soldiers gifts. It's all a little like Halloween in the United States. When the boys were returned to their homes, people celebrated with a big party. Today, los Inocentes is more like April Fools' Day. People play tricks on each other, or try to fool them into believing stories that aren't true.

Party time in Hatillo

The little town of Hatillo has a specially big celebration for los Inocentes. The whole town takes part in a big parade. Everyone gets dressed up in special costumes with masks. Afterward, there's a big party in the public square. This celebration was brought to Puerto Rico from the Canary Islands by people coming from there.

Another tradition for los Inocentes is for people to try to climb a greased pole.

The little town of Hatillo celebrates los Inocentes with a big parade.

Three Kings Day

On January 6, Catholics celebrate the arrival of the Magi, or Three Kings, at the manger of the baby Jesus. Wooden statues of the Three Kings are put up in front of the capitol building in San Juan. Older Puerto Ricans may still gather at a neighbor's house to pray together and to honor the three Wise Men, but today this is a holiday that is mostly for the children. Traditionally, Three Kings Day was the day when Catholics received presents. Although today many people have adopted the U.S. custom of exchanging gifts on Christmas, most still have a few gifts to open on January 6.

Wooden figures of the Three Kings.

Grass for the camels

The night before, children gather fresh grass and place it in shoeboxes under their beds for the Kings' camels, who will be tired and hungry after their long journey. Children believe that the Magi reward good children by replacing the grass with gifts. Their parents might also put out a few pastries for the Wise Men. The children wake up in the morning and excitedly check the boxes to find out what the Kings left for them. They might also find their shoes filled with nuts and candy. Then they quickly dress and go out to watch or join the procession. Children in San Juan then flock to the old fortress, El Morro, to collect free candy and toys.

Children dress up as the Magi to participate in the parade.

Las Octavitas

Many people prolong las Navidades beyond Three Kings Day, for the eight days of adoration of the baby Jesus, called *las Octavitas* [lahs oak-tah-VEE-tahs]. During this time, parents and godparents exchange visits, sing, and recite rosaries—and, of course, continue with more parties, eating, and drinking. It is a tradition that if you receive a visit from a friend or relative on Three Kings Day, you are supposed to return the visit eight days later. The name *Octavitas* means "little eights," meaning eight days after January 6.

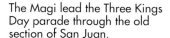

Think about this

Puerto Ricans borrow ideas for festivals from all over. They took ideas for masks and music from West Africa. Many dances and costumes come from Spain. Even the Canary Islands contributed a way of celebrating a festival!

The Magi lead the Three Kings Day parade through the old section of San Juan.

PATRIOTIC FESTIVALS

The Taino people who first lived in Puerto Rico called their island ***Boriquén*** [boh-ree-KAIN]. Puerto Ricans today often refer to themselves as ***Boricuas*** [boh-REE-kwas]. Although Puerto Rico has never been an independent country, there is much patriotic feeling among Puerto Ricans both on the island and in the United States. Many people would like to see an independent Puerto Rico. Others just want to celebrate their homeland and its traditions. Whatever their opinion, there are many occasions to show off their pride in their homeland and their hope for the future.

Shout for freedom

On the night of September 23, 1868, a group of rebels marched into Lares. They took over the town and arrested the mayor. The next morning, they declared the Republic of Puerto Rico. The rebellion later failed, but it was the closest Puerto Rico came to declaring its independence. On September 24, the small town of Lares celebrates the *Grito de Lares* [GREE-toh day LAH-rays] as the birth of Puerto Rico's independence from Spain.

Above: A statue of Ramón Betances, who inspired the Grito de Lares rebellion.

Left: A Puerto Rican man showing his patriotism.

New York goes Boricua

There are many Puerto Ricans in the United States, and most of them live in New York City. Many Puerto Ricans in the United States have never lived in Puerto Rico, but they are still proud of being Puerto Rican. It's fitting that they have their own holiday to celebrate their heritage. In New York City, June 9th is Puerto Rican Day. The day explodes with parades, banners, and drum majorettes marching in time to a Caribbean rhythm. In 1992, the parade included more than 100,000 marchers, and more than 1,000,000 people watched —it was the largest Puerto Rican Day parade in history.

New Yorkers celebrate Puerto Rican Day with a big parade.

THINGS FOR YOU TO DO

The *coquí* [ko-KEE] is a little tree-frog that is found only in Puerto Rico. Its song can be heard at night all over Puerto Rico, and it has become a favorite symbol of the island. The song of the coquí is the only natural song that is a perfect seventh (that's a special musical combination). Maybe the unusual musical talent of the coquí has had an effect on Puerto Ricans—Puerto Rico has certainly produced a lot of music for such a small island, and that music is famous all over the world. Would you like to try your hand at a little music, too? Use the coquí for inspiration, make yourself some maracas, and add a little music of your own to your fiesta!

Make some maracas

Maracas are usually made from a gourd that is carved and stained for decoration and then mounted on a stick, but you could make some out of papier-mâché. Blow up a small balloon. Cover it with a few layers of papier-mâché and let it dry. Then pop the balloon. Put some beans or seeds inside (test it to make sure they make a nice sound). Then put a stick in the hole to make a handle and seal it with papier-mâché. When it's dry, paint your maracas in nice, bright colors. You're ready to play!

Percussion galore

The Puerto Ricans are great inventors of musical instruments. They have three different kinds of guitar—with three, four, or six strings. But they're fondest of percussion instruments. Like the *güiro* [GWEE-roh], a notched gourd played by drawing a stick across it. This instrument originally came from the Tainos. A hollowed tree trunk beaten with sticks also comes from the Tainos, as do maracas. In fact, Puerto Ricans can take practically anything and make a rhythm with it. It's a talent that has been passed down from their African ancestors, and it gives spice to all their music.

Things to look for in your library

Discovering the Music of Latin America (video).
Juan Bobo: Four Folktales from Puerto Rico. Carmen T. Bernier-Grand (Harpercrest, 1994).
Los Pleneros de la 21: Somos Boricuas, Bomba y Plena en Nueva York (CD).
Puerto Rico: From Sea to Shining Sea. Dennis and Judith Bloom Fradin. (Children's Press, 1995).
Puerto Rico: Portrait of America. Kathleen Thompson (Steck-Vaughn, 1996).
Salsa: Latin Pop Music in the Cities (video).
Siembra. Willie Colón and Ruben Blades (Fania Records, 1978).
Teaching the Music of Six Different Cultures (book and tape).

MAKE A VEJIGANTE MASK

P uerto Rican maskmakers usually use a coconut shell to make vejigante masks, but you can make a good one using papier-mâché. Then you'll be ready to join in the fun at Loíza for the feast of Santiago Apostol.

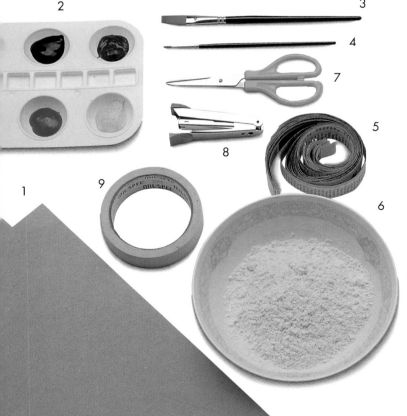

You will need:
1. Two pieces of cardboard 11¹/₂" x 14" (29 x 35 cm)
2. Tempera paints
3. A medium paintbrush
4. A small paintbrush
5. Strips of newspaper
6. 3-4 tablespoons flour
7. Scissors
8. Stapler
9. Masking tape

1 Cut a cardboard circle 10" (25 cm) across. At the bottom of the circle, make a cut 3½" (9 cm) long. Toward the top, make two diagonal cuts about 2" (5 cm) long.

2 Overlap the edges of the lower cut 3" (8 cm) and staple. Overlap the edges of the top cuts 1" (2.5 cm) and staple. Stir the flour into 2 cups (480 ml) warm water, making a thin paste. Dip the strips of paper in the flour paste and apply. Cover the mask with two or three layers of papier-mâché. Let dry.

3 Cut the second piece of cardboard in half lengthwise. Roll each piece into a long, narrow cone, and hold with tape. Cover with several layers of papier-mâché.

4 Cut out eyes and a mouth. Make small cuts in the base of the horns. Papier-mâché the horns to the mask, adding several layers. Let dry.

5 Paint your mask in bright colors. Vejigante masks usually have colors like green, red, orange, yellow, purple, and black, often with dots all over. Attach a piece of elastic and wear it with pride!

Make Besitos de Coco

T hese chewy little cookies are called *Besitos de Coco* [bay-SEE-tohs day KOH-koh], which means "Coconut Kisses." Try them—they'll make your fiesta extra special!

1 Measure all the ingredients into a large bowl and mix them together using the wooden spoon.

2 Pick up a spoonful of the batter and roll it into a ball. Continue until you've used up all the batter. You should have about 24 balls.

3 Grease a baking tray with butter or shortening. Preheat the oven to 350°F (180°C).

4 Spread the balls out on the greased baking tray. Put them in the oven. Be very careful, and be sure to use a potholder (ask an adult to help you with this). Bake them for 30–40 minutes, until they're golden brown.

GLOSSARY

asalto, 19	A surprise parranda.
bomba y plena, 14	A dance that combines African and Spanish elements.
Boricua, 24	Popular name for Puerto Rican.
Boriquén, 24	Original Taino name for Puerto Rico.
conquistador, 13	Conqueror; name for Spanish conquerors of the New World.
cuatro, 18	A small guitar; also groups playing traditional music.
la Isla, 16	Name for Puerto Rico used by U.S. Puerto Ricans.
parranda, 19	Going door-to-door singing Christmas carols.
Paso Fino, 9	A type of Puerto Rican horse that is very graceful.
patron saint, 8	A saint who is supposed to take care of a town.
salsa, 11	Music that combines jazz with Afro-Caribbean percussion.
Taino, 4	The original inhabitants of Puerto Rico.
vejigantes, 15	Masqueraders who wear devil masks for festivals.
Yoruba, 13	A West African tribe, ancestors of many Puerto Ricans.

INDEX

MIAMI
THEN & NOW

ARVA MOORE PARKS
& CAROLYN KLEPSER

Thunder Bay
P·R·E·S·S

San Diego, California

Thunder Bay Press
An imprint of the Advantage Publishers Group
THUNDER BAY 10350 Barnes Canyon Road, San Diego, CA 92121
P · R · E · S · S   www.thunderbaybooks.com

Produced by Salamander Books,
an imprint of Anova Books Company Ltd.,
10 Southcombe Street, London, W14 0RA, United Kingdom

"Then and Now" is a registered trademark of Anova Books Ltd.

ISBN-13: 978-1-59223-875-0
ISBN-10: 1-59223-875-0

The Library of Congress has cataloged the original Thunder Bay edition as follows:

Parks, Arva Moore, 1939-
       Miami then & now / Arva Moore Parks & Carolyn Klepser.
              p. cm.
       ISBN 1-57145-852-2
       1.Miami (Fla.)--History--Pictorial works. 2. Miami (Fla.)--Pictorial works. I. Title:
Miami then and now. II. Klepser, Carolyn. III. Title.
       F319.M6 P373 2002
       975.9'381'002--dc21

                                    2002028924

Printed and bound in China

1 2 3 4 5 12 11 10 09 08

ACKNOWLEDGMENTS
The authors wish to thank everyone who helped with this book, particularly the following: Sam
Boldrick at the Miami-Dade Public Library, Steve Bovo at Hialeah Race Course, Carrollton
School, Steve Chatelaine at the Surf Club, Regina Dodd, Kathleen Dorkowski at Mount Sinai
Medical Center, Julio Grabiel at Spillis Candela, the Grafton Family, Sheila Hellman, Argelio
Hernandez at Miami-Dade County, Dawn Hugh at the Historical Museum of Southern Florida,
Megan Kelly at Swire Properties, the Mandarin Oriental, Hank Morrison, Robert Parcher at the
City of Miami Beach, Laura Pincus, Ransom Everglades School, Anuca Valverde, Nellie Vega for
the Fisher Island Club, and James P. Wendler.

PHOTO CREDITS
The publisher wishes to thank the following for kindly supplying the "then" photographs for this
book on these pages: 6 and 8, Ralph M. Munroe Collection, Historical Museum of Southern
Florida; 10, 14, and 16, Thelma Peters Collection, Arva Parks & Company; 12, 20, 24, 26, 34, 36,
40, 42, 54, 58, 66, 102, 110, 112 (inset, top), 122, and 132, Arva Parks & Company; 18, Daley
Highleyman Collection, Arva Parks & Company; 22, Black Archives; 28, 32, 62, 72, 74, 76, 78,
80, 106, and 116 (right), State of Florida Photographic Archives; 30, 92, 94, 114, 116 (left), 126,
134, and 136, Matlack Collection, Historical Museum of Southern Florida; 38, 70, 82, and 84,
Miami News Collection, Arva Parks & Company; 44, 46, and 142, City of Miami; 48 and 56,
Patty Catlow Collection, Arva Parks & Company; 50, Kate Stirrup Dean Collection, Arva Parks
& Company; 52, Merrick Collection, Arva Parks & Company; 60, Alice Wood Collection, Arva
Parks & Company; 64, 86, 88, 90, and 140, Romer Collection, Miami-Dade Public Library; 68,
Don Kuhn Collection, Arva Parks & Company; 96, LeGro Collection, Historical Museum of
Southern Florida; 98 and 112 (main picture), photographs by Claude Matlack, for Mr. Thomas J.
Pancoast, Miami Beach (now in the collection of Marty Pancoast Grafton); 100 and 124, City
Clerk's Archive, City of Miami Beach; 104 supplied courtesy of the Fisher Island Club; 108, Pete
Chase Collection, Arva Parks & Company; 118, Jay Spence Collection, Historical Museum of
Southern Florida; 120, Mary McIsaacs Collection, Historical Museum of Southern Florida; 128
and 130, Wendler Collection, State of Florida Photographic Archives; 138, Curt Teich Postcard
Archives, Lake County Discovery Museum, Wauconda, Illinois.

Thanks to Simon Clay for taking all the "now" photography in this book, with the exception
of the photographs on the following pages: 11, 23, 67, and 85 (inset, top), courtesy of Arva
Moore Parks; 13, 15, 19, 21, 45, 47, 91, 97, 129, 131, and 143, David Watts; 119, courtesy of
Carolyn Klepser; 37, courtesy of Argelio Hernandez, Miami-Dade County; 81, courtesy of © Dan
Forer; 101, kindly supplied by the Mount Sinai Medical Center; 103, kindly supplied by the
Fontainebleau Hilton.

Page 1 shows Miami Beach, then (photo: © Bettmann/CORBIS).
Page 2 shows: Miami Beach as it looks today (photo: © Buddy Mays/CORBIS).

INTRODUCTION

"From all sorts and kinds of reasons we have come here, but we stay because
we believe tremendously in this place and its future."

Marjory Stoneman Douglas, 1922

No other place is like Miami. It's the nation's youngest major city and its only subtropical megalopolis. Vibrant, alive, and constantly changing, the city attracts all kinds of people. The first arrived more than 10,000 years ago and built settlements on the bay and on a river they called Mayami. The land was theirs for thousands of years until the Spanish sailed in and claimed it for themselves. Bahamian seamen, adept at salvaging the remains of ships that crashed upon the Great Florida Reef, left their island homes and made new ones in south Florida. The Seminole tribe fled the white man's advancing civilization and arrived in Florida, determined to stay. After the United States acquired Florida from Spain in 1821, U.S. soldiers tried and failed to dislodge them from their Everglades home.

Without roads or even trails, the future city of Miami was a nameless, barely inhabited, and mostly unwanted terra incognita when Julia Tuttle arrived from Cleveland in 1891 to claim her 640-acre purchase on the north bank of the Miami River. Her nearest neighbors, William and Mary Brickell, ran a trading post on the other side of the river. They had been there for twenty years and owned more than 2,500 acres of undeveloped land. A few other brave pioneers lived on a scattering of barely improved homesteads and in three small settlements—Coconut Grove, Lemon City, and Cutler. Across the bay, only the House of Refuge, a government life-saving station for shipwrecked sailors, stood sentinel over a failed coconut plantation.

While most saw only an inhospitable, impenetrable, mosquito-infested jungle, Julia Tuttle predicted that the area's geography guaranteed it would someday become a great international city. With a pledge of frost-free winters, half her land, and a promise of more from the Brickells, she convinced Henry Flagler to extend his railroad to Miami, lay out a town, and build a luxury hotel. The first train arrived in April 1896 and by July, 344 men, a third of whom were black, incorporated the instant "Magic City" of Miami.

In the early years of the twentieth century, Miami lost its raw, frontier atmosphere. It began to take on the appearance of a respectable small town that each winter transformed itself into a lively tourist haven. Besides the tourists, Miami also attracted northern industrialists who turned the Brickells' grand new avenue into a "Millionaires' Row." James Deering, a farm machinery magnate, built the beautiful Villa Vizcaya on 180 acres of bayfront land and launched an architectural style that remains popular today.

Carl Fisher, another Brickell Avenue millionaire, invested in a half-finished causeway that connected John Collins's avocado-growing enterprise to the mainland. As part of the deal, Collins transferred a large swath of beach real estate to Fisher. In 1915, Miami Beach became the second south Florida city created to please the tourists.

By all normal standards, Miami was a perpetual boomtown. In the 1920s, the word "boom" even became a proper noun. The Florida Boom even rivaled the 1849 California gold rush for national attention. Almost overnight, the city quadrupled its population, changed its skyline, and exploded its borders.

Of the many legendary developers, George Merrick was in a class by himself. He created Coral Gables—south Florida's first totally planned community. It had a Spanish/Mediterranean theme, complete with beautiful entrances, plazas, and wide boulevards. Phenomenally successful, the development further boosted the popularity of Miami.

Other developers joined in the frenzy and created a variety of fantasy subdivisions, each with a different architectural theme. Not to be outdone, Carl Fisher built luxurious hotels on Miami Beach, as well as other amenities like polo fields and golf courses to please his ever-increasing cadre of millionaire visitors and residents. For a while, it seemed that the Boom would last forever—until nature accelerated the inevitable bust with a killer hurricane. After the disaster of September 17–18, 1926, northern headlines proclaimed: "Miami Is Wiped Out." It was barely an exaggeration.

By the time the 1929 stock market crash plunged the nation into depression, Miami and Miami Beach had already suffered three years of economic ruin. By the mid-1930s, however, while the rest of the nation continued to wallow, more than a hundred new hotels and apartment buildings with stark Moderne lines began to rise on Miami Beach. Although no one knew it at the time, these buildings would not only lead Miami out of depression, they would also become the heart of the world-famous Art Deco District that sixty years later would bring the area international fame.

During World War II, the U.S. Army Air Force took over most of Miami Beach's hotels and apartments and the Navy moved into Miami. Fisher's and Merrick's glamorous hotels became hospitals, posh golf courses became drill fields, and ritzy clubs became mess halls.

After the war, Miami boomed again when thousands of veterans returned to start new lives under the warm sun. Growth continued unabated into the 1950s. Miami Beach welcomed a string of glitzy new luxury hotels and kitschy motels. Miami spread out in all directions.

When Fidel Castro took over Cuba in 1959, no one had any idea that the Castro revolution would change Miami as much as it would Cuba. During the next twenty years, more than half a million Cubans came to south Florida. At first they flocked to an older Miami neighborhood called Riverside, changing it into a vibrant "Little Havana." From this launching place, the Cubans ultimately transformed Miami into the great international city that Julia Tuttle predicted. Other refugees from Latin America and the Caribbean sought out Miami's hospitable shores, adding their own special magic to what was becoming an increasingly cosmopolitan city of constantly changing faces.

Today Miami is thriving on change. The skyline is once again filled with construction cranes as another new Miami emerges and another "now" turns into a "then." No longer at the end of something, Miami is at the middle of everything—the connector of the Americas and the center of an exciting new world.

Arva Moore Parks

In 1884, Ralph M. Munroe, south Florida's first photographer, shot this earliest known photograph of Miami's oldest structure. Built on Key Biscayne in 1825, the Seminole tribe attacked and burned it in 1836. The structure was rebuilt in 1847, with an additional twenty-six feet added in 1855. Confederate guerillas destroyed the lens during the Civil War and the beacon remained dark until 1867. When the Fowey Rock light went into service in 1878, the Cape Florida light was extinguished.

Purchased by the State of Florida in 1966, the lighthouse has been listed on the National Register of Historic Places since 1971. In 1988, Dade Heritage Trust, Miami-Dade County's preservation organization, began a grassroots movement to completely restore the deteriorating structure. Completed in 1996, its public reopening coincided with Miami's centennial celebration. Today it is the focal point of Bill Baggs Cape Florida State Park.

When Ralph M. Munroe took this photograph in the 1880s, the long building on the left served as a trading post and the Dade County Courthouse. South Carolinian William F. English built both structures in the 1840s at the conclusion of the Second Seminole War. When renewed hostilities with the Seminoles forced him to abandon his property, the U.S. Army returned, reactivated Fort Dallas, and completed the two stone buildings for their own use.

In 1925, the Miami Women's Club and the Daughters of the American Revolution launched Miami's first preservation effort to save what was known as Fort Dallas. They moved the building upriver to Miami's Lummus Park, where it remains today. Although it served as part of Fort Dallas from 1849 to 1857, its first use was as quarters for William English's slaves. It is also Miami's first "coral rock" building.

Left: A dense, tropical hardwood forest covered much of the land that would become downtown Miami. After William and Mary Brickell purchased more than 2,000 acres on the south side of the Miami River in 1871, people called the tangled jungle the "Brickell Hammock." This 1890s view shows the Coconut Grove Trail that linked the pioneer community to the Miami River. In the future, this pathway would become Brickell Avenue.

Right: Brickell Avenue is Miami's most glamorous commercial street. While Henry Flagler platted narrow streets on his side of the river, William and Mary Brickell had a bolder vision. They built this beautiful boulevard in 1911 and turned it into Miami's first "Millionaires' Row." Rezoned for high-rise buildings in the 1950s, the homes have been replaced with modern skyscrapers. A monument to Mary Brickell can be seen on the median.

In January 1897, Henry Flagler's grand Royal Palm Hotel opened. It was a huge "Flagler Yellow" mansard-roofed building—five stories tall and almost 700 feet long. Its twinkling electric lights—Miami's first—made it stand out as a veritable fairyland in the midst of the raw, infant city. Damaged by the 1926 hurricane, it was torn down in 1930 and the site became a parking lot.

At night, the Magic City lives up to its name. Lofty towers radiate a palette of glimmering colors. With the wave of a wand, the Bank of America Tower (left), designed by I. M. Pei, changes its evening glow to match the season. Built in 1987, this three-tiered, forty-seven-story structure was the first skyscraper to incorporate an elevated metro station—the Knight Center Station. Not to be outdone, the 764-foot Wachovia Financial Center (center) casts its nightly spell across the bay. Originally known as the Southeast Bank Center (1984–1992) and then the First Union Financial Center (1992–2003), the building was the tallest skyscraper in the southeastern United States when it opened in 1984.

Miami's first grammar school, seen here, opened in 1897. In 1911, the school board built a new concrete building that housed grades one through twelve. A hotelier purchased the old wooden school, moved it to Third Street and Miami Avenue, and transformed it into the Frances Hotel. The federal government acquired the school property in 1931 and tore down the 1911 building to clear the site for a new Federal Courthouse and Central Post Office.

The old Federal Courthouse and former Central Post Office has been called "a monument to three artists"—Phineas Paist, Harold D. Stewart, and Denman Fink. The neoclassical design is influenced by the Mediterranean Revival style made famous by Paist and Fink in Coral Gables. Dedicated on July 1, 1933, its walls are clad in limestone.

The building was listed on the National Register of Historic Places as part of Federal Courthouse Square on October 14, 1983. The tall buildings are the Federal Detention Center (right of center) and the James Lawrence King Federal Justice Building (right).

Left: In 1905, Canadians Salem and Emily Graham built the Halcyon Hotel from locally quarried oolitic limestone. For years, people mistakenly believed that Stanford White, the legendary New York architect, designed the building. Mrs. Graham reportedly said that White only did a quick rendering of the facade on the back of an envelope. In 1937, after years of ups and downs, the DuPont National Bank Corporation bought the property and demolished the hotel.

Right: Sometimes called "Miami's Rockefeller Center," the Alfred I. DuPont Building, designed by the Jacksonville architectural firm Marsh and Saxelbye, opened with great fanfare in October 1939. Nearly 35,000 Miamians passed through the doors of the notable Depression Moderne building on opening day and ogled the impressive brass bas-relief elevator doors and the lavishly decorated ceilings.

In 1911, Locke T. Highleyman developed Point View, one of Miami's first exclusive neighborhoods. He was the first to dredge up the bay bottom to create new land from mangroves. Local luminaries like Frank Shutts, owner of the *Miami Herald,* and millionaire winter residents like William H. Luden, of cough drop fame, built impressive mansions on what is today Brickell Bay Drive—still one of Miami's most beautiful streets.

Today all the mansions are gone and the bayfront is filled with luxury high-rise apartments, hotels, and condominiums. Zoning and lifestyle changes doomed the large estates and elegant homes. One by one, they came down and new owners built modern skyscrapers in their place. The Four Seasons Hotel—the top of its blue tower can be seen in the center of this photo—was completed in 2003. Standing 789 feet high, it is the tallest residential building south of New York. In front of the Four Seasons Hotel are the Mark on Brickell and Oakwood Miami apartment blocks; to the left is the luxurious Jade at Brickell, a 526-foot residential building that features a seventh-floor "resort deck" and infinity pool.

In 1916, Margaret Burlingame purchased a five-acre spoil bank and named it Burlingame Island. The island was barely visible to anyone except the Brickells, who lived across the river from Henry Flagler's Royal Palm Hotel (right). For decades, little changed on the scraggy spit of land except its size. When Edward N. Claughton purchased it in 1943 and renamed it Claughton Island, it had grown to twenty acres.

In the late 1970s, Hong Kong–based Swire Properties purchased most of the island, renamed it Brickell Key, and created a master plan that led to the creation of today's unique island community of more than 1,000 residential units and 340,000 square feet of office and retail space. The addition of the five-star Mandarin Oriental Hotel in November 2000 added to the glamour of what has been billed as "America's only downtown island resort." The tall building at the far left is the Three Tequesta Point, named for the Tequesta Native American tribe that settled at the mouth of the Miami River. Carbonell Condominium (right) is named for the artist Manuel Carbonell (1918–), whose landmark bronze sculpture, *The Tequesta Family*, stands at the Brickell Avenue Bridge.

In 1896, Julia Tuttle and Henry Flagler laid out "Colored Town," west of the railroad tracks between today's Northwest Sixth and Twelfth streets. Its bustling Avenue G, seen here in this view from around 1915, had professional offices, more than thirty stores, and the Lyric Theater (the building with the cupola). Built by Geder Walker in 1913, writers called the Lyric "the most beautiful and costly playhouse owned by colored people in all the Southland."

The restored Lyric Theater is the centerpiece of the Historic Folklife Village in the section now known as Overtown/Park West. Led by Black Archives founder Dorothy Jenkins Fields, future plans include further development of the Folklife Village and the revival of the neighborhood as "Little Broadway," its nickname from the 1930s to the 1960s, when it was a popular tourist destination and entertainment and cultural center.

The Miami City Hospital, designed by August Geiger, opened in 1918, just in time for the terrible flu epidemic. Criticized for being "way out in the country," doctors passed a motion asking the administration to fence in the area to keep cows from grazing under the operating room windows. In 1924, soon after the death of beloved pioneer doctor James M. Jackson, the city commission changed the hospital's name to Jackson Memorial Hospital.

Today's Jackson Memorial Hospital, one of the busiest in the nation, is a county-owned hospital and major teaching facility for the University of Miami School of Medicine. The campus also includes such stellar institutions as the Bascom Palmer Eye Institute and the Sylvester Comprehensive Cancer Center. The old hospital, known as "the Alamo," was saved from the wrecking ball in 1977 and moved a short distance to become the centerpiece of the new complex.

When this photograph was taken in about 1922, the impressive new First National Bank Building (left), Miami's tallest and most elegant skyscraper to date, was almost completed. The multiturreted Halcyon Hotel dominated the other end of the block, which was filled with an assortment of real estate offices, banks, stores, and no fewer than four shopping arcades. In the distance, Elser Pier's new electric sign announced the popular entertainment venue.

The First National Bank Building still stands, although it suffers from an insensitive 1960s remodeling. The Alfred I. DuPont Building, which replaced the Halcyon Hotel, marks the end of the block. Elser Pier is long gone, torn down in the 1920s when the bay bottom was pumped up to create Bayfront Park. Currently undergoing beautification, Flagler Street sports new streetlights reminiscent of the classic 1920s style.

Left: In this June 1926 photograph, a Coral Gables Rapid Transit car prepares to turn at SE First Avenue. The Seminole and McCrory hotels, with their tourist-friendly balconies (right), remained as reminders of the Magic City's earlier days. In the distance, the Bank of Biscayne Bay Building added a new silhouette to the constantly changing skyline. Behind it, the skeleton of the ziggurat-topped Miami-Dade County Courthouse, then under construction, is visible.

Right: With the exception of the 1950s Morris Lapidus–designed Ainsley Building (right), this section of today's Flagler Street looks remarkably like it did in 1926. Although the former hotels have a new facade and have lost their balconies, the distinctive roofline remains. Some of the 1920s details survive near the pinnacle of the Biscayne Building, and the peak of the Miami-Dade County Courthouse is still visible just behind it.

Left: The Scottish Rite Masonic Temple, designed by the prominent architectural firm of Kiehnel and Elliott, was dedicated on March 12, 1924. Built at the start of the King Tut Egyptian Revival craze, the unique structure is also Miami's first Art Deco building. During the Depression, it housed the WPA's Federal Theater and became an Army air raid shelter during World War II.

Right: With its striped classical columns and distinctive ziggurat roof, this unique building is still the meeting place for the Masons. Each of the temple's decorative elements has special meaning for them. The massive pillars at the entrance are thirty-two feet high, in reference to their vaulted thirty-two degree honor. Double eagles are used in various places and the symbolic miter and trowel are frequently encountered.

Begun in 1924 and completed in 1925, the old Miami News Tower is one of Miami's most beloved buildings. Governor James M. Cox of Ohio, who bought the paper following his unsuccessful 1920 presidential campaign, hired the New York firm of Schultze and Weaver to design the instant landmark. Patterned after Spain's Giralda tower, it was the first of three Schultze and Weaver south Florida buildings that sported similar pinnacles.

After the *Miami News* moved out in 1957, the building remained vacant until the 1960s, when it took on a new role as a refugee center for hundreds of thousands of Cubans fleeing communist Cuba. Dubbed the Freedom Tower, it became Miami's Ellis Island. It faced an uncertain future until the influential Cuban American National Foundation acquired it and restored it for use as a Cuban museum and enduring symbol of freedom.

Below: The newly pumped-up Biscayne Boulevard was not finished when the devastating 1926 hurricane struck the unsuspecting city. On the morning of September 18, the wide thoroughfare—with ships strewn about like toy boats—looked more like a yacht basin than a street. After the storm, Miami's new skyline, including the Ingraham Building (left), which was still a skeleton, would remain mostly unchanged until the mid-1950s.

Right: Biscayne Boulevard is still one of Miami's most beautiful streets. For a few years after the One Biscayne Tower (center) was completed in 1973, it was the tallest building in Miami and the harbinger of the new skyline. The Metromover that connects the Brickell, Omni, and downtown area opened in 1986. The Arquitectonica-designed American Airlines Arena, seen in the distance, made its debut on the eve of the new millennium.

Left: In 1904, Dade County built its first real courthouse. Constructed from coral rock, the neoclassical two-story building had an impressive dome and an elegant portico reminiscent of a Greek temple. By 1925, it was clear that the twenty-year-old building could not handle the Boom-induced crowds that descended upon it. Because of the crush to record the multitude of real estate transactions, the new courthouse was built around the old one, where business continued as long as possible.

Right: Miamians believed that their impressive skyscraper courthouse, completed in 1928, befitted their recently acquired big-city image. Designed by A. Ten Eyck Brown and August Geiger, the stately neoclassical structure was the Boom's last gasp. For many years, it was Miami's tallest building. Carefully restored in recent years and now listed on the National Register of Historic Places, this building remains a sentinel from the past and a link between the old and the new.

Between 1926 and 1952, the 241-foot *Prins Valdemar* was a Miami landmark on the northern edge of Bayfront Park. It was called "the ship that stopped the Boom" because for a month in early 1926, it capsized and blocked the Miami harbor, causing a shortage of building materials.

Towed to a permanent home on Sixth Street, it remained there, serving as a restaurant and aquarium, until it was dismantled and towed away in 1952.

The state-of-the-art American Airlines Arena opened on December 31, 1999, with the Gloria Estefan Millennium Concert Spectacular. Located just north of where the old *Prins Valdemar* once rested, the Arquitectonica-designed arena brings new life to Biscayne Boulevard.

At the rear overlooking Biscayne Bay is Gloria and Emilio Estefan's pineapple-topped Bongos, a tropical-themed Cuban café well known for its fine food and hot dancing.

Riverside was Miami's first subdivision west of the Miami River. One of its most prominent landmarks is the imposing Firestone service station. Built in 1929 under the personal supervision of Harvey S. Firestone, who had a mansion on Miami Beach, it was billed as the largest Firestone facility in the world and was considered his favorite store. It also sported the largest neon sign in Florida.

Although Riverside has been transformed into a vibrant Latin Quarter and many of its historic buildings have been demolished, the Firestone service station still dominates the corner of Flagler Street and Twelfth Avenue. After the building was sold to Walgreens, preservationists convinced the company to retain the old structure, thus guaranteeing its continued presence as an enduring and beloved neighborhood icon.

A vibrant neighborhood shopping area grew up on Miami's portion of the Tamiami Trail (SW Eighth Street). Restaurants, shops, and mom-and-pop stores lined the busy street. One of the trail's most popular gathering places was the Tower Theater, built in 1926. In 1931, the Wolfson-Meyer Theater Company (Wometco) hired architect Robert Law Weed to transform it into a little Art Deco gem. The renovation launched Weed's career as a noted theater architect.

After the arrival of the Cuban refugees in the early 1960s, the trail became known as Calle Ocho—the heart of Little Havana. The City of Miami has recently restored the Tower Theater and refurbished Domino Park (left), a popular enclave for elderly Cubans who enjoy playing the traditional game. Each March, the Calle Ocho Open House brings more than a million people to the area for a lively Latin street festival.

When this photograph was taken in 1951, the Port of Miami, seen here, was located at the site of today's Bicentennial Park. The main terminal was little more than a warehouse (right). The bay was filled in after the port moved to Dodge Island in 1965. The Miami skyline—from the distinctive Miami News Tower (right) to the cluster of Biscayne Boulevard hotels (left)—had changed little since the late 1920s.

Today's skyline bears no resemblance to the earlier view. The stern of a cruise ship dominates the tip of a greatly enlarged Port of Miami on Dodge Island—the busiest cruise ship port in the world. The old Miami News Tower, now the Freedom Tower, is barely visible behind the new American Airlines Arena (right), and the soaring County Administration Building dwarfs the Miami-Dade County Courthouse. In Miami, "only the sky is changeless."

When the Spanish arrived in 1566, a Native American village occupied the north bank of the Miami River (left), which would become Miami 330 years later. From the city's earliest days, visitors took riverboats, like the *Jungle Queen* seen here, to visit Native American tourist attractions upriver. Most of the buildings in this 1940s view, except the Alfred I. DuPont Building (left), have been torn down and replaced with new buildings or parking lots.

Today both sides of the Miami River are filled with modern skyscrapers. The Metrorail bridge, built in 1984, arcs over the still-active working river. The First Union Tower—the tallest building on the left—sits on land that was once part of Flagler's Royal Palm Park. The riverfront Hyatt Regency Hotel and James L. Knight Conference Center rise on Julia Tuttle's former homesite. The building to the right is Brickell on the River, a forty-two-floor luxury apartment block that was completed in 2006. With its central downtown location, it offers some of the best views over Miami.

Commodore Ralph M. Munroe, a sailboat designer from Staten Island, was one of Coconut Grove's founders. In 1891, he designed and built this home that he named the Barnacle. He was so pleased with the design that when his family grew, he simply jacked up the first floor to become the second and built a new first floor underneath. In 1911, three years after the "house raising," he added the semiattached, one-story library.

Thanks to the Munroe family, the Barnacle, which is listed on the National Register of Historic Places, remains one of Miami's most treasured landmarks. In 1973, Munroe's daughter Patty and his son's widow, Mary, spurned developers who offered top dollar for the land and instead sold it for less to the State of Florida. Only at the Barnacle can you reenter the "Era of the Bay"—the time before the railroad arrived and changed everything.

Charles Avenue was the first street in the first black community on the south Florida mainland. Originally called Kebo, its original residents came almost exclusively from the Bahamas. These early families came to work at the Peacock Inn, a tourist hotel that once stood in today's Peacock Park. St. Agnes Missionary Baptist Church, later called Macedonia Baptist (left), founded by Reverend Samuel A. Sampson, was the first Baptist church in the area.

Today Charles Avenue is filled with many historic buildings and sites.
Although altered, the original St. Agnes church survives as a reminder
of the early days. The descendants of many of the original Charles
Avenue families still live in Coconut Grove. In recent years, the
community, now called West Grove, has come together to celebrate
its roots and preserve its history.

Plymouth Congregational Church traces its history to Isabella Peacock's Sunday school, organized in 1887. Three years later, eighteen Grove pioneers built the Union Chapel on today's McFarlane Road. It became Union Congregational Church in 1897. In 1917, through the efforts of George Merrick, chairman of the board of trustees, Reverend George Spalding, and Mr. and Mrs. Arthur Curtiss James, Union Congregational built a new coral rock church and renamed it Plymouth Congregational.

New York architect Clinton McKenzie designed this beautiful church. Spaniard Felix Rebom, with only a hatchet, a trowel, a T square, and a plumb line, completed the stonework. The 400-year-old front door came from an old monastery in the Pyrenees Mountains. Several other historic structures are on its expansive campus, including Dade County's oldest schoolhouse, several outbuildings from Coconut Grove's former Matheson Estate, and the original Coconut Grove Waterworks.

In 1891, Flora McFarlane, south Florida's first woman homesteader, organized the Housekeeper's Club for the women of Coconut Grove. The club was the philanthropic and cultural voice of the community and helped define Coconut Grove's special character. In 1905, under the leadership of member Mary Barr Munroe, the club launched the movement to preserve the Everglades. The Walter DeGarmo–designed clubhouse, built in 1921, replaced the original 1897 wooden building.

In 1957, the Housekeeper's Club changed its name but not its mission. Shadowed by new high-rise condominiums and threatened by an ever-encroaching highway, the undaunted Woman's Club of Coconut Grove continues to serve the community that spawned it more than 110 years ago. The simple clubhouse, so much a part of Coconut Grove's past, survives as a highly visible community anchor in a sea of turbulent change.

The Coconut Grove Library is the oldest library in Dade County. It was founded in 1895 by the Pine Needles Club, a junior women's club organized by Mary Barr Munroe. It operated out of the upstairs storeroom of Charles Peacock & Sons General Store for six years until Ralph M. Munroe donated the land in 1901, and the men of the community built the new building next to the Union Chapel (left).

The Coconut Grove Library operated independently until 1957, when it became a branch library of what was eventually the Miami-Dade Library system. In 1963, T. Trip Russell designed the current building, incorporating the defining features of the original library into the new structure. Both the American Institute of Architects and the American Library Association honored his design. Although the scene around it has changed, it remains a popular and enduring Coconut Grove institution.

Perched high on the ridge overlooking Biscayne Bay, the Pagoda derives its name from the pagoda-style building built by Paul C. Ransom in 1902. Ransom, a New York lawyer and educator, opened Pine Knot Camp for boys here in 1896. In 1903, he transformed it into the Adirondack-Florida School, the nation's first two-campus boarding school. Students spent the fall and spring quarters in the Adirondacks and the winter quarter in Coconut Grove.

In 1947, the school closed its Adirondack campus but continued operating in Coconut Grove as Ransom School. In 1974, it merged with Everglades School for Girls and became Ransom Everglades. Today the school has two campuses and almost 900 students in grades six through twelve. The beautifully restored Pagoda is considered "the embodiment of the Ransom Everglades tradition" and a living reminder of the school's illustrious past.

In 1912, James Deering, heir to International Harvester, purchased 180 acres of virgin hammock from Mary Brickell. Architect F. Burrell Hoffman Jr. and his associate Paul Chalfin worked closely with Deering to create Vizcaya, a seventy-room Italian villa on the shores of Biscayne Bay. Deering moved into the house in 1916, but five years passed before its expansive gardens, designed by Diego Suarez, were completed.

In 1952, Dade County purchased the estate from the Deering heirs for $1 million and opened it as a museum. Every year, nearly 200,000 people visit this National Historic Landmark. It has also welcomed international dignitaries such as Queen Elizabeth II of England, King Juan Carlos and Queen Sofia of Spain, Presidents Ronald Reagan and Bill Clinton, and Pope John Paul II. In 1994, Vizcaya was the site for the historic Summit of the Americas.

In 1917, John Bindley, president of Pittsburgh Steel, commissioned the firm of Kiehnel and Elliot to design a palatial winter home on a ten-acre tract of bayfront land in Coconut Grove. This beautiful mansion, called El Jardin, is considered one of the earliest and finest examples of Mediterranean Revival architecture in Miami. Bindley's tropical retreat also had lush gardens, elegant outbuildings, and a breathtaking swimming pool.

In 1961, the Society of the Sacred Heart purchased El Jardin and transformed it into the Carrollton School for Girls. Today more than 600 young women from preschool through high school study amid its incomparable splendor. The Bindley house and its historic outbuildings and features are a living study of Mediterranean Revival architecture and a testament to historic preservation and adaptive reuse.

Main Highway and McFarlane Road were the two main business streets in Coconut Grove. In this view, citizens joined in a rousing Armistice Day parade down Main Highway. The building on the left, though altered, still anchors the corner. Sanders Peacock Store, with the second-story balcony, was one of the main general stores in early Coconut Grove. Owner Arthur Sanders was the nephew of Isabella Peacock, the "mother of Coconut Grove."

Today's Coconut Grove is an enduring community of artists, sailing enthusiasts, bohemians, book lovers, and millionaires. Since its founding, it has been known for its lush green environment and "live and let live" philosophy. The Sanders Peacock Store is long gone and CocoWalk, a Mediterranean-themed shopping, restaurant, and entertainment complex, has taken its place. Each February, the Coconut Grove Arts Festival draws thousands of art lovers to the Grove.

When completed in 1931, the Pan American Seaplane Base at Dinner Key, with its daily flights to Latin America and the Caribbean, launched Miami as the "Gateway Between the Americas." Many famous people, including President Franklin D. Roosevelt, flew from here on the "Flying Clippers." Tourists and residents flocked to ogle the ever-present luminaries and enjoy the drama and spectacle of the Clipper's splashdown in Biscayne Bay.

After Pan American Airways abandoned their seaplane operation, the City of Miami purchased the Dinner Key base in 1946 for use as a waterfront park. For several years, the former terminal housed marina offices and a restaurant until the city converted it into the Miami City Hall in 1954. Designed in the Streamline Moderne style by well-known architects Delano and Aldrich, its Art Deco features and waterfront location befit Miami's modern image.

George Merrick, founder of Coral Gables, named the city after his boyhood home, built in 1907. Eight years earlier, his father, Solomon G. Merrick, a Congregational Church minister in Massachusetts, purchased a 160-acre homestead that was five miles west of the three-year-old city of Miami. After he and George turned the homestead into a successful grapefruit-growing plantation, his artist wife, Althea, designed this spacious coral rock home for the family.

During the Depression, Ethel Merrick, George's sister, made their home a boardinghouse she called "Merrick Manor." In 1966, W. L. Philbrick purchased the house and formed the Merrick Manor Foundation in an attempt to preserve it. Threatened with decay and demolition, the manor was acquired by the city in 1976. Beautifully restored, it is filled with family memorabilia and the artistic creations of Althea Merrick, her son, Richard, and her brother Denman Fink.

Because George Merrick believed that "beautiful things inspire high ideals in the minds of children," he commissioned the firm of Kiehnel and Elliot to design a grammar school in keeping with his Mediterranean Revival–themed community. Particularly suited to south Florida, its airy classrooms are rimmed by arcaded loggias. The original building was completed in 1923 and the beautiful 600-seat auditorium and a second classroom building were added in 1925.

Listed on the National Register of Historic Places, Coral Gables Elementary continues to serve the children of Coral Gables with more than 750 students currently enrolled in preschool through fifth grade. Located in the middle of a growing international city, the student body reflects the area's diversity. In 1993, the central courtyard was dedicated to Eunice P. Merrick, widow of the city's founder, who was on hand to receive the honor.

Billed as "the most beautiful swimming hole in the world," Venetian Pool was originally a rock pit from which the Merricks quarried the oolitic limestone, or coral rock, used to build early homes. In 1924, artistic advisor Denman Fink turned the eyesore into a Venetian lagoon with bridges, grottoes, and wide loggias. William Jennings Bryan, three-time presidential candidate, frequently spoke here using his silver-tongued oratory to promote Coral Gables.

Now listed on the National Register of Historic Places, Venetian Pool is a living monument to George Merrick and his uncle Denman Fink's original vision for Coral Gables. Generations of local residents and tourists have enjoyed its cool water and inviting architecture. Owned by the city and recently restored, it is arguably the most beautiful and unique municipal swimming pool in the world.

In January 1926, George Merrick and hotelier John McEntee Bowman opened the magnificent Schultze and Weaver–designed Miami Biltmore Hotel, billed as "the last word in the evolution of civilization." Nine months after its much-heralded opening, the 1926 hurricane ushered in an era of hard times. Despite the Depression, the hotel remained open until the Army Air Forces turned it into a hospital during World War II.

After the war, the Biltmore became the Veterans Hospital. In 1968, the Veterans Hospital closed and the building faced sale and demolition. Acquired by the City of Coral Gables in 1973, the hotel underwent its first restoration in 1985. Today the Seaway Corporation that leases the hotel has recaptured George Merrick's vision. Named a National Historic Landmark, today's Biltmore is an unparalleled resort hotel and conference center.

In 1925, George Merrick launched the University of Miami with his gift of 160 acres of Coral Gables real estate and a pledge of $5 million. The first building, a beautiful Mediterranean Revival–style confection, was named for his father, Solomon G. Merrick. Under construction when the 1926 hurricane struck, it remained an unfinished skeleton for the next twenty years.

Despite the hurricane, the University of Miami opened as scheduled on October 15, 1926, in a half-finished apartment/hotel that was located several miles from the abandoned campus. "The Skeleton," as it was fondly called, stood alone and covered in vines until 1946, when the University of Miami moved back to its original campus. In 1946, the university completed the Merrick Building, seen here, in a modern style that was noted in national architectural magazines.

George Merrick built the Colonnade, designed by Phineas Paist and Walter DeGarmo, in 1926 as headquarters for his sales operation. Before it was completed, the Boom ended and with it, Merrick's plans. After his Coral Gables Corporation folded, the building had many uses. During World War II, it was a pilot training facility and parachute factory. It also housed a motion picture studio, a gymnasium, and a bank.

In 1985, Intercap Investments saved and completely restored the Colonnade and connected it to a new Spillis Candela–designed hotel and office building. The original Colonnade's impressively restored rotunda became a community gathering place. The modern four-star Omni Colonnade Hotel recalls the historic ambience of the original building through its furnishings, art, and grill, named after "Doc" Dammers, the legendary salesman and first mayor of Coral Gables.

Coral Gables is known for its beautiful gateways and plazas. One of the most impressive is Puerta del Sol (Gate of the Sun). Designed by architects Walter DeGarmo, Phineas Paist, and artist Denman Fink, Douglas Entrance, as it is commonly known today, was part of a planned Spanish village enclosed on a ten-acre site. Although the village was not completed, city officials dedicated the entrance in May 1927.

In 1968, an application to demolish the Douglas Entrance sparked Coral Gables' first preservation effort. Citizens and architects rallied to save it from becoming a supermarket parking lot. Spillis Candela, one of Miami's oldest architectural firms, completed the master plan for the complex, restored the historic buildings, and designed two new towers around this beautiful central plaza. It is listed on the National Register of Historic Places.

Ponce de Leon Boulevard was one of the main thoroughfares in George Merrick's master plan for Coral Gables. It was filled with strictly mandated Mediterranean Revival buildings that even included service stations (right). The imposing Coral Gables Theater (right) has been demolished and replaced with a modern high-rise. Merrick also built several small hotels, including the Sevilla (left). This street remained mostly unchanged from the late 1920s until the late 1960s.

In the 1960s, after Coral Gables changed its zoning to allow high-rise buildings, the area underwent a dramatic change—a trend that continues today. The Texaco Building (left) was the first high-rise in the commercial district. Except for a few small structures, the tower of the Sevilla Hotel, now the Hotel Place St. Michel (left), is the last defining historic landmark on a street that once had the ambience of a Spanish town.

Except for the beautiful 1928 city hall, George Merrick had barely begun to develop Coral Way when the Boom ended. After World War II, Merrick, along with Rebyl Zain, promoted the idea of transforming the mostly barren street into a high-class, modern "Miracle Mile." The idea took hold and the city abandoned Merrick's Mediterranean Revival requirements. They encouraged more modern designs, including the 1948 Art Deco–style Miracle Theatre (left).

Today, Miracle Mile looks much like it did fifty years ago except for newly planted landscaping in the median that blocks the view of the city hall (*see inset*). In 1995, when the Miracle Theatre was threatened with demolition, the city acquired it and designated the Actor's Playhouse as its resident theater company.

During the Boom, James Bright and Glen Curtiss developed Hialeah. Known for its sporting and gaming facilities, the Hialeah Jockey Club thrived for years before Florida legalized pari-mutuel betting in 1931. After Joseph Widener's $2 million refurbishing, Hialeah Race Course reopened in 1932, billing itself the "Saratoga of the South." Citation won the Flamingo Stakes here in 1948. It is now on the National Register of Historic Places.

Squeezed out by nearby competing tracks, the legendary and still
beautiful Hialeah Race Course saw its last race on May 22, 2001.
Facing an uncertain future, the elegant pavilion, ballroom, three
restaurants, and park grounds are now rented for festivals and social
events. The famous flock of flamingos still lives in the track's infield.

In early 1926, aviation luminary Glen Curtiss announced Opa-locka, the last grandiose project of the Boom. Based on a theme from the *Arabian Nights* and designed by architect Bernhardt Muller, his fantasy subdivision had domed palaces fit for the grandest potentate, surrounded by small homes, each with a distinctive Arabian motif. Nowhere else in America could a person live in a home on Sesame Street with two bedrooms, one bath, and a minaret.

Although Curtiss's vision for a complete Arabian-themed community died with the Boom, many buildings had been completed before the crash. Streets were laid out in the shape of the Islamic crescent moon and named for characters in the *Arabian Nights*. Restored in 1988, Curtiss and Muller's masterpiece, the incomparable Opa-locka City Hall, formerly Curtiss's administration building, survives. Each May, the city hosts the Arabian Nights Festival to celebrate its unique character.

Across Biscayne Bay from Miami, banker brothers J. E. and J. N. Lummus sold land at the south end of the beach as early as 1912. Their property along Ocean Drive became a public park. In the foreground of this 1933 view is Cook's Casino, one of four well-known bathhouses along the shore. The 1927 city hall (left) and the luxurious Roney Plaza Hotel (center) were built in the Mediterranean Revival style.

Sand replenishment has widened the beach considerably, but Lummus Park remains the "front yard" of the Miami Beach Architectural District, placed on the National Register of Historic Places in 1979. Lummus Park was added to the National Register of Historic Places in October 2006 and is part of what is now known as the Ocean Drive Deco District of SoBe (South Beach), which stretches along Ocean Drive from Fifth to Fifteenth streets. The cone-shaped tower (left of center) tops the Loews Miami Beach Hotel. Completed in 1998, this 790-room hotel incorporates the 1939 St. Moritz Hotel, which has been fully restored to its Art Deco splendor.

Avery Smith, who came to Miami from Connecticut, built this house in 1918. When he first explored the deserted oceanfront jungle, he said he felt like Robinson Crusoe. Seeing the area's potential, he created the Biscayne Navigation Company, which operated excursion cruises and provided daily ferry service between Miami and the beach. He later purchased and operated Smith's Casino, the beach's first bathhouse that had been built by the unrelated Dick Smith.

The house is built of local oolitic limestone, or coral rock, a popular and inexpensive early building material. Few such structures have survived. In recent years, this little house has been the venue for various restaurants and a beauty spa. Because it is such a rare example of early vernacular architecture and because of its link to Avery Smith, it is a regular stop on walking tours.

In order to transport his avocado crops to the market, John S. Collins, an elderly Quaker from New Jersey, created the Collins Canal in 1912, linking Indian Creek to Biscayne Bay. In 1924, the canal inspired this Venetian-style residence complete with gondolas. The house originally served as a model to promote a planned bayfront cooperative apartment called Villa Biscayne, designed by Schultze and Weaver.

Villa Biscayne was never built, but the famous portrait artist Henry Salem Hubbell made the model his home for several years. Today jet-skiers swoop past the house, unaware of its illustrious past. Now split into rental apartments, it is a highlight of the Palm View Historic District, designated by the City of Miami Beach in 1999 as an enclave of exemplary residential architecture from the 1920s to the 1950s.

In addition to his canal, John S. Collins built a wooden bridge across Biscayne Bay—the beach's first connection to Miami—in 1913. The elegant "Venetian Way," which was interspersed with islands dredged from the bay bottom, replaced the old bridge in 1926. This view looking toward Miami during the causeway's construction shows Trinity Episcopal Church (center) and August Geiger's 1926 Spanish Renaissance–style building for the Miami Woman's Club and Flagler Memorial Library (far right).

The Venetian Causeway and its islands are still a popular route and residential neighborhood. On the Miami side, the Miami Woman's Club Building, its future uncertain, is dwarfed by towering hotels and condominiums. The church, now Trinity Cathedral, is still intact but not visible here. The Miami Herald Building (left) was designed by Naess & Murphy in 1959, modeled after their Chicago Sun-Times Building. In front of the Marriott Biscayne Bay Hotel, on the right side of the causeway, is the Sea Isle Marina, which hosts an international boat show every February. The Venetian Causeway was rededicated in November 1999, following a $29 million restoration project.

In January 1924, John S. Collins's grandson J. Arthur Pancoast opened the elegant Mediterranean Revival–style Pancoast Hotel, Miami Beach's first grand oceanfront hotel. Its architect, Martin L. Hampton, designed many notable buildings in Palm Beach, Miami, and Coral Gables, as well as Miami Beach. During World War II, the Pancoast served as a military hospital. It was demolished in 1953.

Designed by Melvin Grossman and completed in March 1956, the
Seville Hotel is an outstanding remnant of Miami Beach's exuberant
postwar boom. New, glamorous resort hotels abandoned the pedestrian
scale and symmetry of the Art Deco style and outdid one another with
rakish angles, bright lights, and fantasy themes. The Seville is now a
highlight of the Collins Waterfront Historic District, designated in 2001.

Carl Fisher, a self-made millionaire from Indianapolis, was Miami Beach's greatest early developer. He built five hotels, and the Nautilus, on Biscayne Bay at Forty-third Street, was one of the grandest. Designed by New York architects Schultze and Weaver and completed in 1925, it had its own polo fields (right), radio station, and rental cottages on Collins Island (foreground). Fisher built no hotels on the oceanfront, and sold his lots there to his millionaire friends for their private estates.

The Nautilus became a military hospital during World War II and never returned to use as a hotel. In 1946, the local Jewish community established Mount Sinai Hospital, which moved into the vacated Nautilus Hotel in 1948. The Julia Tuttle Causeway (foreground) gave Miami Beach another bridge to Miami in 1959. As Mount Sinai Medical Center expanded, the outdated Nautilus building was demolished in 1968.

Oilman James Snowden was one of Carl Fisher's real estate partners. In the early 1920s, he built this mansion (foreground) on the beach at Forty-fourth Street, then just within the northern city limits. It was the southernmost estate on "Millionaires' Row" that extended north to the Bath Club at Sixtieth Street. Tire magnate Harvey Firestone purchased the home in 1924 and it became better known as the Firestone Estate.

After World War II, all the mansions on Millionaires' Row were demolished in favor of luxury high-rise apartments and resort hotels. In 1954 the Firestone Estate was the first to fall, but a new landmark replaced it—the Morris Lapidus–designed Fontainebleau Hotel.

Reviled by architecture critics at the time, it was an immediate hit with tourists and became an icon of Miami Beach glamour and glitz. It has been a Hilton Resort since 1978.

The 1905 opening of Government Cut severed the southern tip of the beach and created an island that developer Carl Fisher later acquired. In 1925, William K. Vanderbilt II, president of his great-grandfather's New York Central Railroad, built a winter estate here with a mansion designed by Palm Beach architect Maurice Fatio. Vanderbilt traveled the world on his yacht, the *Alva*, seen here, to study marine life. The County (now MacArthur) and Venetian causeways are in the distance.

Since the mid-1980s, Fisher Island has been developed as a private club, inn, and luxury condominium village accessible only by boat, seaplane, or helicopter. The original mansion now serves as a clubhouse, restaurant, and ballroom. The 216-acre island has six restaurants, its own post office, firehouse, bank, market, a nine-hole golf course, and a luxury spa. Residents use golf carts for quiet transportation.

To attract young, active tourists to Miami Beach in the 1920s, Carl Fisher invested heavily in sports—especially polo, golf, and speedboat racing. His first golf course originally extended from Lincoln Road northward to Twenty-eighth Street. August Geiger, Fisher's favorite architect, designed this clubhouse in 1916. It is nearly identical to the Miami City Hospital ("the Alamo") that he designed a year earlier.

Today, the Miami Beach Convention Center occupies what was the southern half of the golf course, but the original clubhouse still stands on the south bank of the Collins Canal at Twenty-first Street. It is a locally designated historic site and one of the oldest buildings in the city. In recent years it has served as an art school for the Bass Museum and as a community theater.

Carl Fisher built Miami Beach's first public school in 1920. Before it opened, Miami Beach children either attended private schools or took the long trip across the bay to public schools in Miami. H. George Fink, George Merrick's cousin and later a prominent Coral Gables architect, designed this Mediterranean Revival–style school with open arcades to take advantage of the ocean breezes.

August Geiger designed many later additions to the original school, including a high school named for Carl Fisher's mother, Ida. Now also named for Leroy D. Fienberg, a principal in the 1960s, Fienberg-Fisher Elementary School has students from fifty countries in preschool through sixth grade. The arcades are still pleasant, and air conditioners were added in the 1960s. The original decorative friezes along the parapet have not survived.

Newton B. T. Roney created this two-block stretch of exotic fantasy in 1924. Roney, a lawyer from Camden, New Jersey, moved to Miami in 1918 and became prominent in banking and real estate. Espanola Way, also known as Roney's Spanish Village, was planned as an artists' colony. Architect Robert A. Taylor designed its shops, apartments, and hotels in pure Mediterranean Revival style. The following year, Roney would open his landmark Roney Plaza Hotel at Twenty-third Street.

In later years, Al Capone's gambling syndicate operated from Espanola
Way, and Desi Arnaz is said to have started the rumba craze here. The
1980s television series *Miami Vice* used this atmospheric street as a
ready-made set. Today, it remains a favorite Miami Beach locale and
still has a bohemian flavor with art galleries, shops, outdoor cafés, and
street festivals. A youth hostel occupies one of the original hotels.

Mangrove forests covered most of the beach when Carl Fisher began creating his winter playground for other wealthy northerners. His Lincoln Road was cleared around 1912 (*see inset*) and soon became the town's social center. The tall building in the 1927 view was designed by August Geiger in 1924 for Fisher's own realty office. The Dowling Building (far left) housed Bonwit Teller and later, Saks Fifth Avenue. Across the street, the Bastian Building contained small shops and offices.

In 1960, architect Morris Lapidus redesigned Lincoln Road as one
of the nation's first pedestrian malls. After a severe economic slump,
restoration efforts in the 1980s began to revive it. Fisher's office
building, now the Van Dyke, houses a popular restaurant and jazz
bar. The Dowling Building has been beautifully restored.

As early as the 1920s, Lincoln Road, with its fashionable shops, was called "the Fifth Avenue of the South." Besides the latest merchandise, the stores also showed off their architecture—using it as a form of advertising. This building was the 1929 showroom, or "salon," for Cadillac, Fleetwood, and La Salle automobiles. Over the door, a carved bas-relief of cars, airplanes, lightning bolts, and the Cadillac crest exuberantly celebrated the machine age.

For decades, plaster cladding had hidden this forgotten frieze—the earliest
example of Art Deco yet identified on Miami Beach. Renovations in
June 2000 brought it back to light. This is one of several Lincoln Road
buildings that now incorporate restored elements from the 1920s into
twenty-first-century additions.

Above: In 1928, architect Alexander Lewis designed a pair of Mediterranean Revival–style commercial buildings on the 900 block of Lincoln Road that faced each other across a courtyard. This Packard showroom occupied part of the eastern building and was one of several elegant automobile salons on Lincoln Road. Both Lewis and another architect, Victor Nellenbogen, had their offices in this complex.

Above: In 1941, Victor Nellenbogen fused the two original buildings into a single Art Deco–style structure called the Sterling Bulding. The original courtyard became an arcade enclosed in front by a second-story wall. The Russian Bear restaurant was an early tenant.

Mitchell Wolfson Jr., founder of the Wolfsonian/FIU, restored the Sterling Building in 1986, launching the revival of Lincoln Road. The Russian Bear is still the name of a café in the building, which also houses a bookstore and other shops and offices. Its blue-and-white facade with a neon-lit swath of glass block is a local landmark.

Early in 1942, as the nation mobilized for World War II, Miami Beach became a major training center for the U.S. Army Air Forces. Tourists left and 85 percent of the city's hotels became barracks. By 1945, the city had hosted half a million troops—both new recruits in ninety-day training and combat veterans who came here for processing and reassignment. The streets, including Lincoln Road, seen here, rang with marching feet and singing soldiers.

Today cyclists and in-line skaters whisk along the old marching route.
John S. Collins's grandson, architect Russell T. Pancoast, designed the
Mead Building for Bonwit Teller in 1928. Its pointed arch has been
reconstructed as an entrance to a Victoria's Secret store.

Joseph Eisener, Carl Fisher's former salesman, built the Deauville Hotel in 1925. It was a gaudy hotel and entertainment complex that boasted Florida's largest swimming pool. But its remote location on the empty beach at Sixty-seventh Street hindered its success. Bernarr Macfadden, a health and diet guru known for outlandish publicity stunts, leased it in 1936 and ran it as the Macfadden Deauville health spa.

The old Deauville was demolished in 1956 and in its place, Melvin Grossman designed the new Deauville Hotel. With its soaring carport, marble lobby, glass-walled dining room, shopping arcade, and even an ice-skating rink, it was the epitome of the glamorous postwar Miami Beach resort-style hotels. A long list of celebrities performed here, including the Beatles in 1964. The hotel, now the Radisson Deauville Resort, retains most of its 1950s architecture.

Henri Levy was a French Jewish immigrant who started a movie theater chain in Cincinnati. He moved his family to Miami Beach in 1922 and soon joined in the real estate boom. One of his developments, named for his homeland, was Normandy Isle in Biscayne Bay at Seventy-first Street. This fountain in a central plaza was one of the first structures built there, lending an air of French elegance to a largely deserted island.

The streets of Normandy Isle still have French names, but most of today's residents are Hispanic. From its inception, a number of factors have hampered the development of this section of Miami Beach, but the area is now undergoing a renaissance. The Normandy Isle Fountain has been adopted as a neighborhood icon and the surrounding plaza is the setting for a farmers market and various cultural events.

For Miami, the heady days of the Boom came to an end on September 17–18, 1926, when a monster hurricane with peak winds of 132 miles per hour pummeled the area. More than one hundred died and thousands were injured. Sand was two feet deep all along Ocean Drive and hundreds of buildings, like the Roosevelt Apartments (left and center) and its neighbor, the Coronado (right), suffered heavy damage.

Buildings that survived the 1926 hurricane are special treasures in Miami Beach today. The Roosevelt, designed by Martin Hauri in 1925, also weathered Hurricane Andrew in 1992. Since then, Miami-Dade County has enacted stringent new building codes. The Roosevelt was extensively renovated in 1993 and is now a condominium with no trace of its past troubles.

In 1927, Martin L. Hampton designed this grand Mediterranean Revival–style building on Washington Avenue to serve as Miami Beach's second city hall. The city had outgrown the first—a small frame building on Fifth Street—and Carl Fisher intended for this impressive structure to restore confidence in Miami Beach after the previous year's devastating hurricane. The north wing originally served as the city's main fire station.

This building no longer serves as city hall but houses court facilities and other offices. The present Miami Beach City Hall was built in 1975 on Seventeenth Street. Old City Hall was beautifully restored in 1987 by Borelli, Frankel, Blitstein Joint Ventures, which at the same time designed the new police headquarters (left), using updated Art Deco design elements.

Left: This 1935 view from the city hall tower evokes the atmosphere of a small tropical town landscaped with palms and Australian pines. Washington Avenue, two blocks west of the ocean, is Miami Beach's main commercial street and was once the trolley route to Miami. In the distance, the Roney Plaza Hotel with its Spanish Baroque tower, designed by Schultze and Weaver, dominates the skyline.

Right: Washington Avenue has undergone many changes. The drumlike building with the green roof (left) at the corner of Thirteenth Street is the 1937 Art Deco–style post office. Although the old Roney Plaza was demolished in 1968, the round pyramidal turret of the Loews Miami Beach Hotel (top right), designed by John Nichols and completed in 1999, serves as a new local landmark. The yellow-topped building to its right is the 2002 Arquitectonica-designed Royal Palm Crowne Plaza Resort.

Drexel Avenue is at the lower right in this 1940s view. The twelve-story Blackstone Hotel (top right), built in 1929, was one of the few large hotels that catered to a Jewish clientele. The white building beneath it is the Astor Hotel, built in 1936. The small coral-rock house (center right) was the home of Henri Levy, developer of Normandy Isle. The Washington Storage Company (left) opened in 1927 and expanded from three to five stories in 1936.

The Washington Storage Building, with two stories added in 1992, is now the Wolfsonian/Florida International University and houses the Mitchell Wolfson Jr. collection of 1885–1945 decorative arts. The Blackstone and Astor hotels are intact. The Drexel Avenue block is now a Best Western Hotel complex, including Henri Levy's house and the Davis Hotel (center right), designed in 1941 by Henry Hohauser. The towering condominiums in the distance are at the southern tip of Miami Beach. To the left is the high-rise Jade at Brickell Bay, a luxury condominium completed in 2004.

Much to the dismay of local residents, gangster Al Capone moved to Palm Island a few years after it was created from the bay bottom. He bought a house here in 1928 and added an above-grade swimming pool and this loggia, or pool house, the following year. Although Capone was involved in local bootlegging and gambling operations, he strove to maintain a normal family life. Here, in 1930, his son hosts local children at a backyard birthday party.

When Al Capone went to prison in 1931, his family continued to reside in the Palm Island home. After his release, Capone lived out his last years here as an invalid and died in the house in 1947. The main house, two-story gatehouse, pool, and this loggia remain as a private residence and a popular attraction on sightseeing tours.

The Collins-Pancoast family had set aside some of their land for a public park even before Miami Beach was incorporated. The John S. Collins Memorial Library is seen here being dedicated in Collins Park on February 26, 1931, as the city's first public library building. Collins's own grandson, Russell T. Pancoast, designed the building. In 1937, sculptor Gustav Bohland added friezes of local scenery over the doors.

The Collins Library was rededicated as the Bass Museum of Art in 1964, housing the fine arts collection of John and Johanna Bass. The building has had several expansions, most recently Arata Isozaki's avant-garde 2001 addition (*inset*). The Collins Park neighborhood is now being revitalized. In addition to the Bass, a new building for the Miami City Ballet and a proposed regional library will complete the cultural campus.

In 1930, one hundred wealthy beachgoers formed their own club at Ninetieth Street, beyond the Miami Beach city limits. Architect Russell T. Pancoast designed the elegant clubhouse that soon became a mecca for the social set. Fearing that the City of Miami Beach would annex their domain, on May 18, 1935, Surf Club members persuaded local residents to incorporate Surfside and lent the town its first year's operating budget.

Winston Churchill stayed at the Surf Club several times and enjoyed painting by the ocean. Still an elegant private club, the original clubhouse is intact, with dining rooms, a ballroom, a pool, cabanas, and twenty-six hotel rooms open only to the Surf Club's 350 members and their guests. Surfside remains a low-rise residential neighborhood, with the taller buildings of Bal Harbour beyond.

Left: A symphony of horizontal and vertical elements, with its curved, ribbed corner and towering neon-sign pylon, the 1939 Tiffany Hotel is a masterpiece of tropical Art Deco designed by Miami Beach's master architect L. Murray Dixon. The futuristic architecture of the 1939 New York World's Fair clearly influenced its design. Soon after its completion, it became one of the hundreds of "barracks hotels" for World War II trainees.

Right: Today this beautifully restored building is a gem in the historic district. But the Tiffany has lost its name. When the famous jewelry company sued the hotel for trademark "dilution," local preservationists lobbied Congress to pass legislation in November 1999 that protects any designated historic property from such lawsuits. But it was too late for the Tiffany. The pylon still stands, but the hotel now does business as simply "The Hotel."

Miami Beach's revolutionary Art Deco architecture used simple geometrical shapes and common building materials in imaginative ways. Here, opposite Lummus Park (right), two Art Deco–style hotels, the 1939 Winter Haven (far left), designed by Albert Anis, and the 1938 Crescent (center), by Henry Hohauser, flank the more traditional Mediterranean Revival–style Edgewater Beach Hotel, designed by Roy F. France in 1935. France also designed the Art Deco–style St. Moritz (center) in 1939.

At the north end of Ocean Drive, the Winter Haven and other reminders of the irrepressible spirit of Depression-era Miami Beach line the way to an enclave of the city's newest twenty-first-century architecture: Arquitectonica's Royal Palm Crowne Plaza; the Loews Miami Beach Hotel, incorporating the restored St. Moritz; Ocean Steps; Michael Graves's 1500 Ocean Drive; and Il Villaggio. This is Miami—then and now—the best of both worlds.

Nothing shows off Miami's magic better than its luminous skyline reflecting on a mirror bay. In this late 1940s view, the pinnacle of the Everglades Hotel (middle), once Miami's finest, serves as a centerpiece for the Magic City. Soon after this picture was taken, workmen turned it into a nondescript hulk when they chopped off its tower to accommodate the antennae of WTVJ, Florida's first television station.

As night falls, the Magic City comes alive, throwing jewels of many colors across the water—reflecting in the glow. From Brickell to Bayside, stately silhouettes vie with each other for attention. As the sky darkens, the city's ever-changing skyline illuminates the stage for the next Miami that waits impatiently in the wings, preparing to emerge. Prominent buildings on the horizon include the fifty-five-story Wachovia Financial Center (left of center), which was the tallest building in Miami when it was completed in 2004; 50 Biscayne (center), which opened in 2007 and can be identified by its brightly lit tenth floor that contains an infinity pool in tropical landscaping; and the Bank of America Tower (right of center), which is illuminated in different colors depending on the time of year.

INDEX